D0034528

Sky Surfing

by Pat Ryan

Content Consultant:
Joe Jennings
Professional Sky Surfing Camera Flyer
Parachute Industry Association

CAPSTONE BOOKS

an imprint of Capstone Press
Mankato, Minnesota

Capstone Books are published by Capstone Press
151 Good Counsel Drive, P.O. Box 669, Mankato, Minnesota 56002
http://www.capstone-press.com

Library of Congress Cataloging-in-Publication Data
Ryan, Pat.
    Sky surfing/by Pat Ryan.
    p. cm. -- (Extreme sports)
    Includes bibliographical references and index.
    Summary: Describes the history, equipment, and techniques of the relatively new sport that involves a team of skydivers, one surfing and one filming.
    ISBN 1-56065-537-2
    1. Skysurfing--Juvenile literature. [1. Skysurfing. 2. Skydiving.]
    I. Title. II. Series.

GV770.23.R93 1998
797.5'6--dc21

        97-11337
        CIP

        AC

Editorial credits
Editor, Timothy Larson; Cover design, Timothy Halldin; Photo Research
  Assistant, Michelle L. Norstad
Photo credits
Brian Erler, 26, 34
Brent Finley, 4, 16, 28, 30, 32, 36
FunAir Productions/Michael McGowan, cover, 6, 9, 10, 12, 14, 18, 20, 22, 24, 38, 40, 47

2 3 4 5 6 05 04 03 02

Table of Contents

Chapter 1
Sky Surfing

Sky surfing is a team skydiving sport. Skydiving is the sport of jumping from an airplane with a parachute. A parachute is a large piece of strong, light fabric. A parachute allows a skydiver to float slowly and safely to the ground.

A sky surfing team is made up of a sky surfer and a camera flyer. Team members fall as far as possible before opening their parachutes.

A sky surfer rides a board that looks like a large snow ski. The board is called a skyboard. A camera flyer photographs and videotapes a sky surfer's ride. Cameras are mounted on a camera flyer's helmet.

A sky surfer rides a skyboard by standing on it. A sky surfer does tricks while riding the board. A sky surfer stays on the board with the help of bindings. Bindings are straps or mechanical devices that attach a sky surfer's shoes or boots to

A sky surfing team is made up of a sky surfer and a camera flyer.

Sky surfing team members wear parachute packs on their backs.

a board. Sometimes, a sky surfer removes the board before landing.

Most sky surfing teams jump from altitudes of 12,500 feet (3,750 meters) or higher. Altitude is the height of an object above the ground. Team members open their parachutes at altitudes of 3,000 to 2,000 feet (900 to 600 meters).

Free-Fall

Free-fall is the time a sky surfing team falls before members open their parachutes. Free-fall starts when a sky surfing team leaves a plane. It ends when the team members open their parachutes. Free-falls last from a few seconds to slightly more than one minute.

A sky surfing team falls towards the ground in different positions. Team members fall faster and faster until they reach the fastest free-fall speed. This speed is called terminal velocity. Most teams have terminal velocities of 110 to 120 miles (176 to 192 kilometers) per hour. A team reaches terminal velocity in about 10 seconds.

The sky surfer begins a routine once the team exits the airplane. A routine is a planned series of sky surfing tricks. Tricks include rolls, flips, and spins. At terminal velocity, the sky surfer has a sense of being weightless. The weightless feeling helps the sky surfer move more freely. The sky surfer has about 50 to 60 seconds to finish a routine.

The Parachute

The sky surfer and camera flyer store their parachutes in packs. The packs attach to the team members with harnesses. Sky surfing teams wear parachute packs on their backs.

The sky surfer and camera flyer wear altimeters. An altimeter is an instrument that shows the altitude of a falling object. Some altimeters are worn on the wrist. Others are attached to parachute packs worn on the chest.

The sky surfer and camera flyer usually deploy their parachutes at about 3,000 feet (900 meters). Deploy means to put into action. Team members check their altimeters to know when they are at 3,000 feet. At this altitude, they pull rip cords on their parachute packs. A rip cord is a thin rope or wire that deploys a parachute when pulled.

Many sky surfing teams use altitude warning devices and automatic activation devices (AADs). An altitude warning device is a loud beeper. It reminds team members to deploy their parachutes. An AAD is a device that automatically deploys a parachute at a set altitude. An AAD will deploy a parachute even if sky surfing team members cannot.

Extreme Sky Surfing

Skydiving and sky surfing are extreme sports. Sky surfing team members must be highly skilled

A sky surfer and a camera flyer usually open their parachutes at 3,000 feet (900 meters).

skydivers. Errors or problems with equipment can be deadly. Many athletes consider these sports the most difficult extreme sports. An athlete is someone trained in a sport or game.

There are sky surfing competitions. A competition is a contest between two or more athletes. Competition gives sky surfing teams a chance to show their skills. Competition also shows people that sky surfing is a serious sport.

Chapter 2
The History of Sky Surfing

People have had ideas about safely jumping from great heights for hundreds of years. Some people wrote about their ideas. A few daring people tested their ideas. Some of these ideas and tests led to today's sport of sky surfing.

The Early Thinkers

People thought about parachutes long before airplanes were invented. The Chinese were the first people to think about parachutes. They came up with ideas for parachutes more than 1,000 years ago.

The Chinese drew pictures of parachutes shaped like umbrellas. An umbrella is a device with a covered, dome-shaped frame and a handle. An umbrella protects people from the rain or the

Sky surfing is the product of many people's ideas about skydiving.

Jean-Pierre Blanchard tested parachutes by dropping dogs out of a hot air balloon like this one.

sun. No one knows if the Chinese ever made or tested their parachutes.

In 1494, Italian inventor Leonardo da Vinci had an idea for a parachute. Da Vinci drew pictures of the parachute. He wrote about how it would work.

Da Vinci's parachute was supposed to be large, triangle-shaped, and made of cloth. Experts believe da Vinci never had the chance to make his parachute. But some of today's parachutes are shaped like the one he imagined.

The Balloon Jumpers

Jean-Pierre Blanchard was a Frenchman. He lived during the 1700s. Blanchard believed that people with parachutes could jump safely from hot-air balloons. A hot-air balloon is a large balloon filled with hot air. It also has a basket for carrying passengers.

Blanchard designed and built a hot-air balloon in 1784. He also made cone-shaped parachutes. Blanchard strapped his parachutes to dogs. Then he dropped the dogs from his balloon. Experts believe the dogs survived. No one knows if people ever used his parachutes.

In 1797, Frenchman Andre-Jacques Garnerin became one of the first people to use a parachute. Garnerin parachuted from a hot-air balloon over Paris.

Garnerin attached an open parachute to the balloon's basket. He rode the balloon to an altitude of 3,000 feet (914 meters). Then Garnerin cut the basket away from the balloon. The parachute helped Garnerin float safely to the ground inside the basket.

Today's parachutes and parachute packs are the product of early tests by Leslie Irvin.

The Improvers

In 1887, tightrope walker Tom Baldwin invented a parachute and harness. The harness was a new feature. It attached an open parachute directly to a person. Baldwin tested his parachute by jumping from a hot-air balloon. He made a safe landing.

Charles Broadwick invented the canvas parachute pack in the early 1900s. Broadwick folded and stored his parachute in the pack. He strapped the pack to his back.

Broadwick jumped from a hot-air balloon wearing his pack. Then he pulled his parachute from the backpack. Broadwick scared and thrilled people who were watching the jump. At first, they thought he had no parachute. Broadwick landed safely.

In 1919, Leslie Irvin tested a new kind of parachute and pack. His parachute had a rip cord. People were afraid that jumpers would pass out before pulling their rip cords. But Irvin proved that these parachutes were safe and easy to use.

In 1925, Steven Budreau became one of the first people to experiment with long free-fall. He fell 3,500 feet (1,050 meters) before opening his chute. Budreau used different body positions to control his speed during the free-fall. He inspired people to experiment with different free-fall positions.

Today's skyboards are patterned after the first modern skyboard.

The Skydivers

Experts disagree about who made the first parachute jump from a plane. Some say that Grant Morton made the first jump in 1912. Others say it was Captain Albert Berry in the same year. Experts agree that Georgia Tiny Broadwick was the first woman to jump from a plane. She made her jump in 1913.

During the 1920s, aviation grew quickly. Aviation is the science of flying and building airplanes. Interest in skydiving also grew. People tested new kinds of parachutes. They developed different skydiving skills.

Many countries relied on skydiving as part of their military operations during World War II (1939-1945). After the war, military skydivers continued to skydive. Skydiving caught on as a sport. It remains a popular sport today.

The Sky Surfers

In 1980, some people experimented with new ways of free-falling. During free-fall, they laid down on small surfboards called boogie boards. But the boards were hard to control. This made them too dangerous to use.

True sky surfing began between 1988 and 1990. Skydivers tested boards that could be ridden while standing up. By 1990, skydivers had invented the modern skyboard. The board looked like a short, wide snow ski. It was safe and controllable. Most of today's skyboards are patterned after this board.

Chapter 3
Skills and Competition

Sky surfers and camera flyers are professional athletes. A professional athlete is someone who receives money for taking part in a sport. A professional also has a high level of skill. Extreme sky surfing teams must use all their skills to complete their routines.

Both the sky surfer and the camera flyer must be excellent skydivers. They both must know basic and advanced skydiving skills. Each team member must know what the other will do while in the air.

Mistakes during free-fall might mean lower scores for a routine. Mistakes can also lead to midair collisions, parachute problems, and even death. To prevent problems, a sky surfing team learns how to work with the wind. Both team

Both members of a sky surfing team must be excellent skydivers.

Sky surfers jump from planes on their boards in the full standing position.

members learn about wind resistance and free-fall methods.

Wind Resistance

Wind resistance is the force of the air that pushes against moving objects. For skydivers, wind resistance provides a slight upward lift on their bodies. This allows skydivers to have a safe period of free-fall.

A sky surfing team takes advantage of wind resistance, too. Wind resistance pushes upwards on a sky surfer's board. This allows a sky surfer to move on the wind. A sky surfer moves on the wind like a surfer moves on a wave.

A camera flyer free-falls like a skydiver. But a camera flyer must use a combination of free-fall methods. These methods help a camera flyer keep up with a sky surfer.

The Sky Surfer's Methods

Sky surfers jump from planes with their boards attached to their feet. They usually start in the full standing position. In this position, a sky surfer stands upright on a board. The full standing position is the basic position for a sky surfer.

All sky surfers learn to sky surf in the full standing position. It requires some practice. At first, new sky surfers tumble around a lot. They have trouble controlling their boards and staying in the full standing position. With practice, this position becomes easier and more natural for new boarders.

Sky surfing tricks include back loops.

Sky surfers perform tricks in the full standing position. They perform tricks by making different body movements. Moving the board also helps sky surfers perform tricks. They combine body and board movements to perform tricks, too.

Tricks include twists, spins, cartwheels, back loops, and helicopters. A spin is a series of twists. A cartwheel is a circular, sideways handstand. A back loop is a wide, backward roll. A helicopter is an upside-down spin. A sky surfer's board spins like the blades of a helicopter during this trick.

The Camera Flyer's Methods

The most common free-fall methods for camera flyers are a series of free-fall positions. The basic free-fall position is the full-stable-spread position. In this position, a camera flyer free-falls facing the ground. The camera flyer's back is well arched and the head is held back. The camera flyer's arms and legs are extended.

The full-stable-spread position gives camera flyers the most control. It keeps them from rolling or spinning out of control. Camera flyers go into different free-fall positions from this position.

Camera flyers can also use the frog position. The frog position is a relaxed version of the full-stable-spread position. In the frog position, the flyer's back remains arched. The knees and elbows are bent.

From this position, a camera flyer is able to make body movements. The movements make the camera flyer quickly change directions. To

Camera flyers can quickly change directions while in the frog position.

turn right, a camera flyer lowers the right arm and shoulder. To turn left, a camera flyer lowers the left arm and shoulder.

A camera flyer goes into the delta position to increase speed. In this position, the camera flyer holds the arms along the body. The camera flyer also pushes outward with the legs. This creates fast forward movement. A camera flyer reaches speeds of 200 miles (320 kilometers) per hour or more in this position.

Extreme Competition

In the 1980s, there were only a few sky surfers. By 1990 there were hundreds of sky surfers. They wanted a chance to compete and show off their sport. In 1990, sky surfers got their chance. They demonstrated the sport during the World Freestyle Championships.

The 1990 World Freestyle Championships introduced team sky surfing. Camera flyers videotaped their partners' routines. For the first time, onlookers were able to clearly see the routines.

The demonstration showed people that sky surfing is a serious sport. This helped sky surfers find sponsors and organize competitions. A sponsor is a person or business that helps organize and pay for an event.

Today, there are thousands of sky surfers around the world. Both men and women compete. They compete against one another during small and large world-class competitions. The

Both members of a sky surfing team receive points for a routine.

SkySportif International (SSI) Pro Tour and the Extreme Games are two of the largest competitions.

SSI Pro Tour

The SSI Pro Tour consists of four competitions. The competitions are held at different locations around the world each year. This allows many sky surfing teams to compete.

During competition, judges score both members of a sky surfing team. The sky surfer's points make up 75 percent of the total score. The camera flyer's points make up 25 percent.

A sky surfer receives points for basic and advanced tricks. Advanced tricks receive more points. A camera flyer receives points based on how well the videotape captures the routine.

Winning sky surfing teams advance from one competition to another. The best teams advance to the Extreme Games at the end of the tour.

The X Games

The Extreme Games is a competition featuring many extreme sports. The games are shown on television. Extreme sky surfing is one of the featured sports.

The Extreme Games are also called the X Games. There are Summer and Winter X Games. Sky surfing is part of the Summer X Games. Sky surfing teams that win at the Summer X Games are considered the best in the world.

Chapter 4
Equipment

Sky surfers in the 1980s experimented with equipment made for water and snow sports. They tried surfboards with snowboard bindings. The equipment did not work well for sky surfing.

Sky surfers realized that sky surfing needed its own equipment. They worked with manufacturers to build and test new boards and bindings. They also tested different kinds of parachutes. The tests led to today's basic sky surfing equipment.

Skyboards

Manufacturers make skyboards out of aluminum and graphite. Aluminum is a light metal. Graphite is a light mineral often used in pencil lead. Aluminum and graphite make the boards light and strong. This helps make the boards stable and easy to use.

Each board has bindings with safety releases. The releases let sky surfers easily remove their board while in midair. Sky surfers will often

Each skyboard has bindings.

A ram-air canopy is made up of sections called cells.

remove their boards in times of danger. This helps them stay in control of their dives.

Some boards also have recovery systems. A recovery system is a small parachute that automatically deploys. The parachute opens as the board falls away from the surfer's feet. Recovery systems allow sky surfers to easily recover their boards. They also keep the board from hurting onlookers or damaging property on the ground.

Manufacturers customize each skyboard for its rider. Customize means to make something to suit individual needs. They often consider a sky surfer's skill level and weight. Each of these determines the size of a board. The average skyboard is less than one inch (2.5 centimeters) thick.

A beginner needs a small board. Smaller people also use smaller boards. A small board is easier to control than a large board. Experienced sky surfers need larger boards. Larger boards help experienced surfers perform advanced tricks.

Parachute Rigs

The standard parachute pack is called a rig. Each rig has a main parachute and a reserve parachute. The reserve parachute is there in case the main parachute does not work properly. Both parachutes are called ram-air canopies. A ram-air canopy is shaped like a rectangle. A canopy is the fabric part of a parachute.

A ram-air canopy works like a wing. It is made up of sections called cells. Air flows through the cells. This allows the parachute to glide on the wind. Gliding helps sky surfing team members land softly and with more control.

Video Recorders and Cameras

Most camera flyers use video recorders and video cameras. Sometimes camera flyers also use still cameras. Video recorders capture routines on videotape. Video cameras broadcast routines as they

Camera flyers wear cameras and video recorders on camera helmets.

happen for televised competitions. Broadcast means to send out a program. Still cameras take individual pictures of moments during a routine.

Camera flyers wear their video recorders and cameras on camera helmets. The camera helmets keep the camera flyers' arms free for free-fall.

Camera flyers start their video recorders and video cameras as their teams leave the planes. Their routines are broadcast to large television screens at the competition site. They are also broadcast to televisions in people's homes. Judges watch the videotaped routines after the sky surfing teams reach the ground.

Sky surfing still cameras have wires attached to them. The wires are attached to remote controls. Camera flyers hold the controls in their hands. They push buttons on the controls to make their cameras take pictures.

Clothing

Sky surfers and camera flyers wear jumpsuits. Sky surfers' jumpsuits have high-drag tops and low-drag bottoms. High-drag tops increase wind resistance. This gives sky surfers more stability. Low-drag bottoms lower wind resistance. This helps sky surfers better control their boards.

Most camera flyers wear low-drag jumpsuits. The low-drag suits allow camera flyers to move and free-fall quickly. Some camera flyers' jumpsuits have thin, fabric wings. The wings run from the wrists of the suits to the waist areas. The wings become firm when a camera flyer's arms are extended. The wings help camera flyers slow down and change directions.

Many camera flyers wear athletic shoes. Some wear boots. The shoes and boots fit tightly into the bindings of their sky boards. Shoes and boots prevent twisted ankles in the air and during landings.

Shoes and Bindings

Skyboard

Altimeter

Parachute Rig and Harness

Camera Helmet

Jumpsuit

Parachute Rig and Harness

Chapter 5
Safety

Some people believe sky surfing is too dangerous. They also believe sky surfing teams are careless thrill-seekers. But this is not the case. Sky surfing teams are always concerned about safety. Collisions, blackouts, equipment failure, and strong winds can be serious problems for team members.

Sky surfing teams understand that being well trained keeps the sport challenging, exciting, and safe. Teams first learn skydiving basics. They also learn about the equipment they use. Then they learn sky surfing basics. Sky surfing teams master moves and tricks. They practice their routines over and over.

Training

People who want to sky surf learn to skydive first. They complete many hours of ground school. In ground school, students learn

Sky surfing team members first learn skydiving basics.

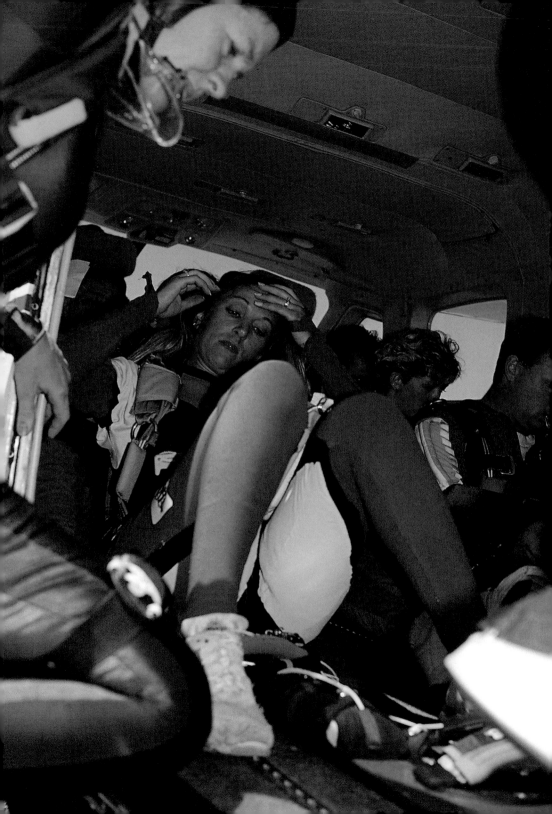

skydiving basics in a classroom. Some basics include free-fall positions and parachute maintenance. Parachute maintenance includes knowing how to check and pack a parachute. Skydiving students even learn some flying skills.

Then students are ready to make practice jumps from airplanes. They practice until they master the basic skills. Skydiving students make 200 practice jumps from planes before they are ready to sky surf.

Sky surfing students take classes before they try the sport. During the classes, students learn how to safely make sky surfing jumps. Camera flyers learn advanced free-fall methods.

Experts teach sky surfing students how to balance on their boards. They teach students how to stay in control of their boards. Experts also teach the students how to deal with emergencies. Sky surfing students then make practice jumps with the experts. The students practice the skills they learned in their sky surfing classes.

Sky surfing students go up in planes to make practice jumps with experts.

Sky surfing teams practice their routines on the ground first.

Practice Makes Perfect

Each sky surfing team member works alone to master skills, moves, and tricks. Then the team members plan a routine together. The routine is made up of selected tricks. The sky surfer and camera flyer agree which tricks should be part of a routine. They only choose tricks they can safely perform and photograph.

Sky surfing teams practice their routines on the ground first. They try to copy what they will do in the air. Sky surfers show camera flyers their routines. Camera flyers practice videotaping and taking pictures from different angles.

Finally, the team practices its routine in the air. Team members make practice jumps together. After each jump, they discuss problems they faced. The team practices until it perfects its routine. Most teams make hundreds of practice jumps before competing.

A Safe Future

Extreme sky surfing teams are working hard to make their sport even safer. Teams learn new safety skills and demand safe equipment. They attend safety meetings.

Skyboard manufacturers work to make equipment that meets the needs of sky surfing teams. Together, manufacturers and sky surfing teams make extreme sky surfing a safe and exciting sport.

Words to Know

altimeter (al-TIM-uh-tur)—an instrument that shows the altitude of a falling object

altitude (AL-ti-tood)—the height of an object above the ground

athlete (ATH-leet)—someone who is trained in a sport or game

automatic activation device (AAD) (aw-tuh-MAT-ic ak-tuh-VAY-shuhn di-VISSE)—a device that automatically deploys a parachute at a set altitude

binding (BINDE-ing)—a mechanical device or a set of straps that attaches a sky surfer's shoe or boot to a sky board

boogie board (BUH-gee BORD)—a small surfboard

competition (kom-puh-TISH-uhn)—a contest between two or more athletes

free-fall (FREE-fawl)—the period of time a skydiver falls before opening a parachute

frog (FROG)—a relaxed version of the full-stable-spread position; a sky surfer's back is arched, the knees and elbows are bent, and the head is upright

full-stable-spread (FUL STAY-buhl SPRED)—the basic free-fall position; a sky surfer free-falls facing the ground, with back arched, head back, and arms and legs extended outward

hot-air balloon (HOT-air buh-LOON)—a large balloon filled with hot air that has a basket for carrying passengers

ram-air canopy (RAM-air KAN-uh-pee)—a modern, rectangle-shaped parachute that works like a wing

skyboard (SKY-bord)—a lightweight board made of aluminum and graphite that looks like a large snow ski

skydiving (SKYE-div-ing)—the sport of jumping from an airplane with a parachute

sponsor (SPON-sur)—a person or business that helps organize and pay for an event

terminal velocity (TUR-muh-nuhl vuh-LOSS-uh-tee)—the fastest free-fall speed for a given skydiving position

wind resistance (WIND ri-ZISS-tuhnss)—the force of the air that pushes against moving objects

To Learn More

Barrett, Norman. *Skydiving*. New York: Franklin Watts, 1987.

Engle, Eloise. *Parachutes: How They Work*. New York: Putnam and Sons, 1972.

Meeks, Christopher. *Skydiving*. Mankato, Minn.: Capstone Press, 1991.

Tomlinson, Joe. *Extreme Sports: The Illustrated Guide to Maximum Adrenaline Thrills*. New York: Smithmark Publishers, 1996.

Useful Addresses

Fédération Aéronautique Internationale
93 Boulevard du Montparnasse
75006-Paris, France

SkySportif International
3740 North Josey Lane, Suite 130
Carrollton, TX 75007

United States Parachute Association
1440 Duke Street
Alexandria, VA 22314

Internet Sites

First Sky Surfing Jump
http://www.parachutehistory.com/skydive/
    firstboard.html

Sky Surfing Club
http://www.users.waitrose.com/~skysurfers

Sky Surfing International
http://expn.go.com/xgames/s/2000/0725/52.html

What It Is!
http://homepage.mac.com/ssiprotour/9what.html

Extreme sky surfing is a challenging and exciting sport.

Index